Winged Wonders

SOLVING THE MONARCH MIGRATION MYSTERY

BY MEEG PINCUS

ILLUSTRATED BY YAS IMAMURA

For centuries, up and down North America,
every year brought a mystery.

Monarch butterflies swooped in for a spell, like clockwork, from somewhere beyond—then disappeared as curiously as they came.

Where do they go?

People pondered from southern Canada...

. . . through the middle of the United States

. . . and all the way to central Mexico.

In 1976, the world finally learned the answer...
with a groundbreaking discovery.

A one-of-a-kind insect journey.
A remote roosting place.
A small speck on the map—
where millions of monarchs are drawn like magnets each winter.

The Great Monarch Migration,

the news stories called it.

MONARCH
JOURNEY
BEGINS

MEXICO

THE GREAT
BUTTERFLY HUNT

HOW TO SPOT
A MONARCH

So, who solved this age-old mystery?

Who tracked these winged wonders from
one end of the continent to the other?

Who found their secret roosting place,
a marvel of nature?

Was it Fred, the Canadian scientist,

who spent 30 years studying the monarch mystery from his university lab,

who drove through the United States with Norah, his research-partner wife, like detectives, trying to track the cagey creatures' migration from Canada southward,

who tagged monarchs' fragile wings—first with paint
that faded, then with labels that plopped to the ground
when wet—and finally with price tags that stuck?

Was it Norah, master organizer
of the monarch material they collected,

who placed ads in newspapers near and far, seeking ordinary
people to help by tagging monarch wings in their hometowns,

who wrote newsletters and kept in touch with all those volunteers,

who logged and mapped every tidbit of information they sent in to the lab?

Was it those dozens
(then hundreds, then thousands)
of science teachers,
backyard gardeners,
and other curious souls

MONARCH MIGRATION

who answered Norah's ads
and became citizen scientists,

who gently caught, tagged, and
released the delicate, dancing insects—

to help solve the migration mystery?

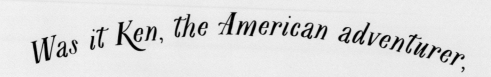

Was it Ken, the American adventurer,

who spotted Norah's ad in a Mexico City
newspaper while visiting there,

who called her in Canada and agreed to follow the monarchs through Mexico, where he didn't speak the language,

who bumped along winding roads with his newlywed wife, Catalina, for nearly two years, trying to track the butterflies' twisting trail?

Was it the villagers and farmers of central Mexico,

who directed the couple to look
higher, higher—up into the thin air
of the volcanic mountains and their
oyamel tree groves,

who for generations welcomed the
monarchs as soaring spirits during
autumn *Día de los Muertos* celebrations,

who held the whispered whereabouts
of their winter roosting place?

Was it Catalina, born and raised in Mexico, who introduced Ken to her beloved monarchs,

who spoke with the locals in her
Spanish dialect to guide their search,

who kept 40 notebooks of meticulous monarch data,

who first crunched through early-morning snow, high in the
Sierra Madre mountains, into an *oyamel* grove, and exclaimed...

"I see them! I see them! Up here!"?

Was it Jim,
the American science teacher,

who, with his students, attached teeny tags to tiny wings,

who caught and tagged the very monarch in a Minnesota goldenrod field that Fred later found among millions in a Mexican *oyamel* grove,

who gave Fred the proof he needed—that one teeny tag—to announce the discovery of The Great Monarch Migration?

YES. THE ANSWER IS YES.

All of them—the scientists, the citizen scientists, the regular folks along the way—played a part in this discovery.

Each person, in small ways or large, helped
answer that centuries-old question:

WHERE DO THEY GO?

And now we know...

Each year, millions of monarchs fly the same path—
generation after generation—
from southern Canada, through the United States,
to roost for the winter in central Mexico's mountains.
Then they journey north again—
feasting on milkweed plants all along the way.

However...

Today, there's a new burning monarch
question to be answered:

How will they survive?

Monarchs' numbers have plummeted since the 1976
discovery. From at least a billion down to millions—
a handful now to each hundred then.

Chemical sprays destroy their milkweed plants.
Logging and farming threaten their *oyamel* groves.
Pollution disrupts the air and weather for their flights.

So, who can make a difference for the monarchs today?

Who can preserve their landing spots and airstreams?

Who can keep them alive?

The answer is actually no mystery at all.

MORE ABOUT the MONARCH MIGRATION "DISCOVERY"

It was in the August 1976 issue of *National Geographic* magazine that Dr. Fred Urquhart revealed his finding of a single monarch butterfly in Michoacán, Mexico, that marked a discovery. Citizen scientists Ken Brugger and Catalina Aguado Brugger had led Fred and Norah Urquhart into that *oyamel* grove, a year after the younger couple found the overwintering site with the Urquharts' guidance. A tree branch heavy with monarchs snapped and fell right in front of Fred, who then spotted that tagged monarch among millions of flapping wings. It turned out that the tag had been affixed to that monarch wing by high school science teacher Jim Gilbert, and two of his students, in Minnesota.

That single monarch provided the proof that Fred and Norah had sought for over three decades, proof of the monarch butterflies' cross-continental, multi-generation migration—one of the longest insect migrations on Earth. Without each person's individual contributions—from Catalina's Spanish and Ken's drive, to the Mexican locals' long-held knowledge, to the thousands of citizen scientists' tagging efforts—the remarkable route of The Great Monarch Migration might still be a mystery to the wider world. It's also important to note that history depends on who tells the story—Mexican poet and environmentalist Homero Aridjis asks: "Did the white scientists really 'discover' the wintering sites that people in Southern Mexico knew about for centuries?" What do you think?

Plenty of mystery continues to surround these delicate but durable insects. Scientists across the continent still study the unpredictable, fluctuating numbers of monarchs migrating each year—in the Great Migration from Canada to Mexico as well as in shorter migrations on the U.S. east and west coasts. Researchers continue to learn more about just how these brilliant bugs make their epic trek.

Citizen science around the monarchs is also still alive and well. After the Urquharts retired their tagging program, University of Kansas professor Chip Taylor started up a new one in 1992—Monarch Watch, which continues to collect data through volunteer citizen scientists. Monarch Watch encourages people to set up Monarch Waystations and informs the public of the monarchs' annual numbers. Other organizations offering monarch citizen science opportunities are The Monarch Larva Monitoring Project and Journey North.

For me, the monarchs' migration route discovery and continuing story illustrate so beautifully how every one of us can have an impact on the world around us. I hope it empowers you—as it does me—to take actions, large or small, to care for our planet and all living beings, like the mysterious monarch butterflies. Each of us doing our own unique part can join together to make a real difference.

For a full bibliography and educational guide, please visit sleepingbearpress.com/teaching_guides.

HOW to HELP the MONARCHS

According to Monarch Watch, "habitats for monarchs are declining at a rate of 6,000 acres a day in the United States." What can we do to change that?

Here are some ideas:

Raise, tag, or report monarchs you see, as a citizen scientist.

Live more lightly on Mother Earth (use less plastic, electricity, water, chemicals; eat more plant-based, local foods).

Plant native milkweed, with no chemical sprays, wherever you live—from a small garden to a larger Monarch Waystation.

Fundraise for or donate to nonprofit organizations that help save the monarchs.

Learn and educate others about The Great Monarch Migration and how to conserve it.

Which of these actions could you take with your family or your class? What part can you play in the continuing story of the magical monarchs?

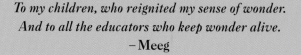

To my children, who reignited my sense of wonder.
And to all the educators who keep wonder alive.
— Meeg

To Andrew, my partner in all adventures and curious pursuits.
— Yas

Special thanks to Angie Babbit, communications coordinator at Monarch Watch,
The University of Kansas, Lawrence, Kansas, for her fact-checking on this book.

SLEEPING BEAR PRESS™
2395 South Huron Parkway, Suite 200
Ann Arbor, MI 48104
www.sleepingbearpress.com

Printed and bound in the United States.

10 9 8 7 6 5 4 3 2 1

Library of Congress Cataloging-in-Publication Data

Names: Pincus, Meeg, author. | Imamura, Yasmin, illustrator.
Title: Winged wonders : solving the monarch migration mystery /
by Meeg Pincus ; illustrated by Yas Imamura.
Description: Ann Arbor, Michigan : Sleeping Bear Press, [2020] | Audience:
Ages 6-10 | Summary: Monarch butterflies swooped through and people
wondered, "Where do they go?" In 1976 the world learned: after
migrating, the monarchs roost by the millions in an oyamel grove in
Mexico. This was a mystery that could only be solved when people worked
as a team— Provided by publisher.
Identifiers: LCCN 2019047136 | ISBN 9781534110403 (hardcover)
Subjects: LCSH: Monarch butterfly—Migration—Juvenile literature.
Classification: LCC QL561.D3 P56 2020 | DDC 595.78/91568—dc23
LC record available at https://lccn.loc.gov/2019047136